Autism and Gastrointestinal Complaints

of related interest

The AiA Gluten and Dairy Free Cookbook
Foreword by Rosemary Kessick, Allergy Induced Autism
Compiled by Marilyn Le Breton
ISBN 978 1 84310 067 6

A User Guide to the GF/CF Diet for Autism,
Asperger Syndrome and AD/HD
Luke Jackson
Foreword by Marilyn Le Breton
ISBN 978 1 84310 055 3

Diet Intervention and Autism
Implementing the Gluten Free and Casein Free Diet for
Autistic Children and Adults – A Practical Guide for Parents
Marilyn Le Breton
Foreword by Rosemary Kessick, Allergy Induced Autism
ISBN 978 1 85302 935 6

Autism, Brain, and Environment
Richard Lathe
ISBN 978 1 84310 438 4

Autism and Gastrointestinal Complaints

What You Need to Know

Rosemary Kessick

Jessica Kingsley Publishers
London and Philadelphia

First published in 2009
by Jessica Kingsley Publishers
116 Pentonville Road
London N1 9JB, UK
and
400 Market Street, Suite 400
Philadelphia, PA 19106, USA

www.jkp.com

The information in this book is not to be construed as medical advice. It is essential
that any ongoing gastrointestinal complaints suffered by anyone be thoughly
investigated by a medical specialist.

Library of Congress Cataloging in Publication Data
Kessick, Rosemary.
Autism and gastrointestinal complaints : what you need to know / Rosemary
Kessick.
p. cm.
Includes bibliographical references and index.
ISBN 978-1-84310-984-6 (pb : alk. paper) 1. Pediatric gastroenterology. 2.
Autism in children--Complications. I. Title.
RJ446.K47 2009
618.92'33--dc22

2008042028

British Library Cataloguing in Publication Data
A CIP catalogue record for this book is available from the British Library

ISBN 978 1 84310 984 6

Printed and bound in Great Britain by
Athenaeum Press, Gateshead, Tyne and Wear

To my beautiful William
whose suffering has
empowered so many parents,
enlightened so many doctors,
and saved so many children from
the pain he had to endure.

With all my love.

Contents

Introduction

Children and adults on the autistic spectrum frequently suffer from gastrointestinal complaints such as diarrhoea, constipation, abdominal pain, abdominal distension, and flatulence.

Far from being 'just part of the condition', worldwide research is confirming that many children and adults on the spectrum with an array of gastrointestinal symptoms are actually suffering from serious underlying conditions which, left untreated, are a source of constant pain that can seriously exacerbate behavioural symptoms.

This book will be of invaluable assistance to teachers, parents, relatives, therapists, nurses and absolutely anyone concerned with the welfare of an adult or child with autism spectrum disorders (ASD). Designed to inform and educate, the initial section summarizes the anatomy and functioning of the digestive system before moving on to highlight specific symptoms associated with gastrointestinal disease and, more particularly, how this manifests within the setting of ASD.

How today's gastroenterologist identifies gut disease is discussed, highlighting state-of-the-art technology followed by practical ways of coping with gastrointestinal problems in the home and school setting.

Case histories illustrate the progress of disease and how it affects the growing ASD child, and a series of useful resources empower the reader to analyse and document any difficulties. Finally, a glossary of common medical terms associated with gastrointestinal diseases explains their meanings in plain English whilst a comprehensive Bibliography of published medical papers completes the book.

1

Understanding Gastrointestinal Complaints in Individuals with Autism

Clinical studies worldwide have demonstrated that combinations of the symptoms described in this section, when seen in autism spectrum disorders (ASD) (including attention deficit disorder (ADD) and attention deficit hyperactivity disorder (ADHD)), more often than not, indicate disease of the gastrointestinal tract which, when treated with the appropriate medication, leads to a significantly better quality of life for the sufferer.

There follows a simplified description of the underlying causes of the symptoms. All these have been described by doctors across the world who have published medical papers based on their clinical evaluations of ASD children and adults. A selection of these papers appear in the Bibliography.

A brief tour of the digestive system

The digestive system (Figure 1.1 on p.13) begins in the mouth where enzymes are released to begin the process of digestion. When food and liquid are swallowed, a flap of tissue called the epiglottis covers the trachea and larynx to ensure that nothing passes into the lungs.

The pharynx is a short tube which doubles up as part of the digestive system and the respiratory system before the parting of the ways at the oesophagus, a muscular tube which moves food down from the pharynx to the stomach.

Once in the stomach, food is broken down by acid before passing through into the small intestine, so-called because its diameter is narrower than the large intestine. Of the two, the small intestine is considerably longer and comprises three parts.

The small intestine is where most of the work is done to extract the nutrients the body needs to function and grow. The first section of the small intestine, leading out of the stomach and about 30 cm long, is the duodenum. As the mulched-up food passes through the duodenum, the gall bladder releases bile to break down fats.

The intestinal muscles move the mixture through the digestive system by way of a series of coordinated contractions called 'peristalsis'.

The pancreas helps the breakdown by releasing more enzymes in addition to insulin which regulates the blood sugar.

The next section of the small intestine, between 1.5 and 2.5 m long, is the jejunum, whilst the end – and longest section at between 5 and 6 m long – is the ileum.

The ileum passes into the first part of the large intestine, the caecum, to which the appendix is attached. The large intestine normally hosts a selection of bacteria which, in the healthy individual, assist in the further breakdown of the mixture.

The next section is the colon, which basically goes up, across and then down. These sections are referred to as: the 'ascending colon', the 'transverse colon' and the 'descending colon'.

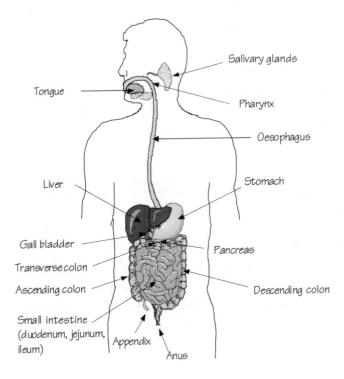

Figure 1.1 The digestive system

Nearly there! The final 15–20 cm form the rectum where the faeces sit ready to exit the body at the anus.

So in, down, round, down, around the squiggly bits, through, up, over, down, through and out…ish!

Signs and symptoms

Many parents and professionals are unsure as to what exactly constitutes a sign or symptom of potentially serious gastrointestinal problems, which is why some ASD children and adults endure prolonged, unrecognized suffering. The following are all indicators that should be taken seriously and investigated appropriately.

Abnormal bowel movements

Many ASD children suffer from diarrhoea, constipation or both. Any consistently abnormal bowel movements indicate that further investigation is warranted.

DIARRHOEA

The most common symptom is chronic diarrhoea; although this is a classic sign of Crohn's disease when it is secondary to chronic inflammation, it is also associated in equal measure with inflammation in autistic enterocolitis.

Frequently, the diarrhoea is the result of disrupted transit time of food through the system and sometimes diarrhoea may be a symptom of an allergy or intolerance to one or more foodstuffs. This, too, is common in ASD.

MUSHY STOOLS

Often, the child or adult has only ever produced mushy, unformed stools. These mushy stools often have a curious grainy consistency, though the reason for this remains a mystery.

CONSTIPATION

Constipation may be obvious, in that the child or adult passes a motion infrequently and has extreme difficulty when they do. Sometimes, however, what appears as a soft mush in the toilet or pad or as soiling in the pants, is confusingly also a symptom of constipation.

Many parents react to this suggestion with disbelief until they see with their own eyes on an X-ray that there is a huge build-up of faeces called a 'faecal mass', and the mush they see is what manages to squeeze past this lump.

The contents of the toilet bowl are very telling. Suspect a problem if you find long strings of faeces or huge solid lumps that block the system. (If it does that to the toilet imagine what it does to the system that produced it!)

Sometimes bits break away, looking like rabbit droppings and sometimes there's an alternation of constipation and diarrhoea. This is not normal and should *never* be put down to the vague term, 'toddler diarrhoea'. (Especially when the child isn't a toddler!)

Sometimes a compacted, dry lump can be huge in comparison to the size of a child. For example, masses the size of a grapefruit have been seen in three-year-olds. Can you imagine how uncomfortable it would be if you had a proportional lump of poo stuck in your innards?

The ASD child or adult who doesn't open his or her bowels on a *regular* basis and who blocks the toilet when they do also has a problem. *This is not normal.*

Undigested food in the stools

A classic symptom of bowel disease is the presence of undigested food in the stools. The lining of the small bowel is damaged and the subsequent disturbance prevents the normal efficient absorption of nutrients as the food passes through the system. Pancreatic or liver disease may also be present, causing malabsorption or quite simply constant diarrhoea owing to overly rapid transit through the system preventing food being absorbed. This malabsorption of food can have severe consequences on the growing child whose body is being starved of the fuel it needs to run the normal metabolic processes so the sight of undigested food in the stools should be taken very seriously indeed.

Odours

There is no delicate way of putting this; the faeces from ASD children are usually extremely malodorous, noxious and plain stinky! The whole digestive system is disordered; the body's enzymes are not being produced as they should, whilst the gut bacteria, which normally work harmoniously with the digestive system, helping to break down waste products, are depleted and disordered. Additionally, there is often a huge build-up of gas which causes further discomfort and pain for the sufferer and howls of protest from bystanders when it's finally released into the atmosphere! As well as the physical pain the autistic person suffers, they are frequently upset by the inability to control these bodily functions and the subsequent embarrassment caused.

Bad breath is also a common symptom; this may be a result of disordered gut bacteria or the slow movement of the faeces along the gut resulting in backflow to the upper digestive system.

Postures

Unable to articulate the pain and discomfort they are feeling, children often adopt positions which are, in fact, a very real way of trying to make themselves more comfortable.

The child who regularly adopts a position with his or her bottom up in the air, higher than the head or lies with an object like a desk corner poking into the lower abdomen is, in fact, trying to take the pressure off in order to relieve the chronic discomfort. They may have discovered that pressing directly above their pubic bone with their hands down their trousers will relieve the pain. Often mistaken for masturbation, their carers make every effort made to prevent the 'behaviour'. Some children will only sleep lying over an object like a gym ball or very large cuddly toy.

Another physical sign of a problem is seen when the child regularly adopts unusual positions on the toilet, for example standing on the toilet bowl and squatting down, knees in the air. In fact the child is doing the most sensible thing by generating intra-abdominal pressure on the cavity in order to help evacuate the bowel. Sadly, this too is often interpreted as purely a 'behavioural' problem in an ASD child or adult who cannot understand the norms expected of him or her.

Distension

Often, but not always, ASD children and adults have distended bellies. This is caused by the inability to pass food through the system efficiently with resultant bloating caused by trapped gas, which in itself can cause pain, or the contents of the stomach not passing through into the top end of the small intestine.

Growth retardation

Another symptom is that of growth retardation. The normal child grows rapidly in terms of their body and their brain function, understanding and cognitive abilities. Cognitive growth tends to go hand in hand with weight gain and the child whose growth is compromised by gastrointestinal malabsorption is an urgent case for referral and treatment.

Blood in the stools

Bleeding can occur when the tissue of the anus is torn by pushing to expel overly hard faeces and this will appear as fresh blood in the pants or the toilet bowl. Dried flecks of blood, however, are different as they can be a sign that there is disease and bleeding further up the gastrointestinal tract. Blood in the stools is known to be a classic sign of colitis, but curiously many ASD children who do have inflammatory bowel disease do *not* have the classic signs of blood in the stools and many doctors have in the past dismissed the patient as a result. It must be stressed that if the signs of pain and discomfort are present the child must be investigated appropriately.

Bladder control

It isn't unusual for the ASD child to lose, or never gain, urinary continence as a result of constipation and/or a reaction to food or an environmental substance. Constipation can in itself cause loss of bladder control and children frequently gain or regain appropriate control once their bowel disease and dietary issues have been addressed.

Mouth ulcers

Crohn's disease can manifest in the mouth and when it does it is generally considered to be secondary to inflammation elsewhere in the digestive system, although there is confusingly also a condition called 'oral Crohn's disease' which shares the same features without the immediate intestinal involvement, which can appear later. ASD children and adults suffering from very painful mouth ulcers, cracked swollen lips, fissures on the sides of the mouth and candida of the mouth should be referred immediately for treatment and the possibility of gastrointestinal inflammation investigated.

Dietary issues

For some ASD children with bowel problems, dietary intervention alone has been reported as rectifying the difficulties and establishing a normal pattern. However, there seems to be increasing evidence from worldwide studies that many ASD children and adults are suffering from an underlying inflammatory condition affecting the whole of the gastrointestinal tract in varying degrees.

Worms

Ongoing infections with worms should be brought to the attention of the doctor. Whilst children often suffer with worms, ASD children are frequently plagued with infestations of all sorts of worms and other parasites, including the bacterium, *Helicobacter pylori*, which is known to be associated with certain types of ulcers in the digestive system.

Polyps

If the ASD child or adult is frequently poking things up his or her nose it could denote the presence of polyps, which are an irritant. A polyp is an abnormal growth that sticks out from mucous membrane. Presence in the nose may denote presence in the mucous membranes in the gut and, on examination, highly inflamed polyps have been found in the gastrointestinal tract of ASD children.

Eating problems

If the child or adult on the spectrum is reluctant to eat or displays challenging behaviours during, before or after mealtimes, it may indicate the presence of gastritis – inflammation of the mucosal lining of the stomach. In the presence of this inflammation, when stomach acid is released in anticipation of and response to food, it causes severe stomach pain, vomiting and reflux.

Self-harm

Constant self-harming, biting, scratching and head-banging are all associated with the severe pain that the ASD child or adult is enduring. The possibility of gastrointestinal disease should always be considered in these cases.

Acid reflux

Many of the children and adults suffer from ongoing acid reflux, causing much pain and discomfort. This should be taken seriously and investigated appropriately.

Puffy eyes

Constantly puffy eyes with dark circles around them may indicate chronic constipation and also allergy or intolerance to certain foods.

Hyperactivity before passing a motion

A frequently observed symptom is marked hyperactivity or aggression or both, just before passing a motion, followed by the total opposite afterwards.

Candida

ASD children and adults often suffer from candida in the mouth; this can be reflected elsewhere in the digestive system and may indicate a compromised immune system.

Coeliac disease

Coeliac disease is not an inflammatory bowel disease but a well-understood condition in which the body reacts to gluten, a protein found in wheat, oats, barley, rye and spelt. It is a permanent hypersensitivity in which the small bowel's ability to absorb nutrients is severely compromised by the flattening of the villi, the frond-like projections on the lining of the small intestine. Permanent removal of gluten from the diet is essential.

Coeliac disease is underdiagnosed and although a potent indicator in children is failure to thrive, many sufferers are asymptomatic. It is also associated with a variety of neurological conditions and, as there is a known genetic component, should always be considered when there is a family history of the condition.

The emerging picture

So, what is beginning to emerge is a pattern of disease in the ASD population where the gastrointestinal tract is diseased and very sick indeed. What is found inside the digestive systems of the children and adults are the following:

- inflammation

- lesions (internal wounds)

- swollen lymph glands (just like the ones in your neck when you are ill) sometimes to the point of causing an obstruction

- inability to properly absorb nutrients necessary for growth because the walls of the intestines lined with villi are flattened or inflamed and can't do their jobs properly; villi are tiny finger-like fronds that protrude from the surface of the intestine and increase the surface area of absorption

- internal bleeding.

All these symptoms cause major pain and discomfort for the non-ASD child, who has a better chance of being able to describe how he or she feels both physically and mentally. The ASD child is far less likely to be able to describe pain, feelings of discomfort or embarrassment or both. The inability to communicate effectively, together with untreated pain, often manifests itself in the child's behaviour.

Children and adults who are able to articulate their pain describe inflammatory bowel disease as 'intolerable', 'white-out', 'inability to concentrate on anything else'. Sadly, many of the estimated 70 per cent of those on the autistic spectrum suffering with gastrointestinal symptoms are just unable to make those who care for them aware of their pain. This inability to communicate often results in aggression, self-mutilation or violence which, in turn, is treated as a behavioural problem as opposed to a treatable, medical disorder.

If you suspect that an autistic child or adult in your care is suffering from any of the symptoms described and they are not being cared for by a gastroenterologist then it is important that you or those with parental or legal responsibility bring the possibility of undiagnosed gut disease to the attention of their GP and/or paediatrician for immediate investigation.

Tragically, many adults on the spectrum have suffered for many years with no one to advocate for them or make the connection between their behaviour and pain. A recent example came to light when an autistic man, who can use a keyboard but neither speaks nor makes eye contact, articulated that he thought he would '...die from the pain'. This gentleman was also able to distinguish clearly between pain caused by excess acid reflux, alleviated by anti-acid medication and the lower abdominal pain experienced when there is inflammation present.

Inflammatory bowel diseases

In one recent study, among an increasing number of studies on the subject, of 145 patients whose condition had merited clinical investigation, 72 per cent were found to be suffering from either an acute or a chronic inflammatory gastrointestinal condition.

Figure 1.2 shows the diagnosed conditions of 145 ASD patients admitted to hospital because of their gastrointestinal symptoms. Some patients suffered from more than one condition and so appear in more than one column.

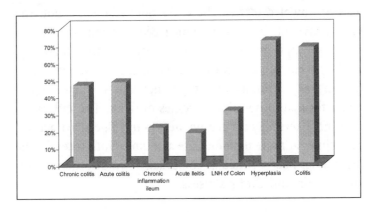

Figure 1.2 Patient analysis

If we look at the study just quoted, the conditions break down as follows:

- chronic colitis, 46%

- acute colitis, 48%

- chronic inflammation of the ileum, 21%

- acute ileitis, 18%

- lymphonodular hyperplasia (LNH) of the colon, 31%

- hyperplasia, 72%.

- any colitis, 68%

Hyperplasia is a chronic proliferation of cells, which in this context indicates an inflammatory response that is not always visible with the naked eye. Biopsy samples, tiny pieces of tissue taken from the gut wall during examination, are examined later under the microscope to confirm the presence of hyperplasia. Seventy-two per cent of the ASD children examined in this study had hyperplasia.

These conditions form part of a constellation of inflammatory bowel diseases. These are not, absolutely not, the same as irritable bowel syndrome (IBS). Inflammatory bowel disease (IBD) is disease of the gastrointestinal tract characterized by recurring episodes of inflammation. The inflammation makes the lining of the gut hot and swollen, painful ulcers form and digestion becomes difficult. The inflammation and ulcers may occur anywhere in the digestive tract and sometimes at more than one site at a time. Until recently, the disease has been defined as comprising two disorders: ulcerative colitis, and Crohn's disease.

Crohn's disease

Crohn's disease is usually characterized by transmural (across walls) inflammation of one or more areas of the digestive tract, with normal areas of gut in between. It can occur anywhere from the mouth to the anus, but most commonly is found in the small and large intestine. This inflammation may lead to ulceration, abscesses and strictures in the bowel. It is a chronic (long-lasting) condition which can wax and wane over a period of months and years. So far there is no cure but treatment can produce a symptom-free remission.

In Crohn's disease the symptoms are extremely variable and can include severe abdominal pain (sometimes mistaken for appendicitis), vomiting, nausea, persistent diarrhoea (possibly with blood and/or mucous), constipation, dramatic weight loss, tiredness, anaemia and mouth ulceration. Sometimes the symptoms may not initially suggest bowel disease at all, with the child or young adult feeling very lethargic with a loss of appetite, skin rash or even a failure to grow; symptoms not normally associated with bowel disease.

Oral Crohn's disease affecting the mouth and lips, occurs quite frequently in children and may occur with or without any involvement of the digestive tract.

Ulcerative colitis

The second widely described IBD is ulcerative colitis, which is inflammation of the *superficial* mucosal layer of the colon (large bowel), causing ulceration and bleeding. Only the large intestine is affected in ulcerative colitis. It may affect only the rectum or may spread along the whole length of the colon (universal or total colitis). It is characterized by periodic relapses, where the symptoms recur and periods of remission, where the patient is symptom-free.

In ulcerative colitis the symptoms are usually more acute, with severe abdominal pain, persistent diarrhoea, usually with blood and mucous (slime) in the stools, and joint pains.

ASD children and adults have been diagnosed with Crohn's disease or ulcerative colitis or both, but often the condition, as seen in ASD children and adults, may appear as a hybrid of the two, sometimes described as a sort of pre-Crohn's state and named 'autistic enterocolitis'.

Medical diagnosis of gastrointestinal disease

Until very recently, the only means of examining the inside of the digestive tract was by inserting a camera on the end of a long wire and pushing. This can be done from the top down or the bottom (literally!) up and is called 'endoscopy'. Now that's a very crude way of describing some very expensive equipment and procedures which, as well as being able to record pictures of what's inside, can also, by means of a nifty device, clip pieces off for examination under the microscope.

This technology has been the mainstay of gastroenterology for some time, but neither the top-down (gastroscopy), nor the bottom-up (colonoscopy), or the two combined, can reach the whole way. In fact, it leaves around 20 feet of the small bowel unexplored, and that tantalizingly inaccessible section proved to be just the area of suspicion in the ASD patients.

It proved impossible to make the endoscopes any longer as they lost all manoeuvrability, and not even special imaging studies like computerized tomography (CT) scan or magnetic resonance imaging (MRI) proved useful in this circumstance. X-rays of the small intestine may be performed after drinking a chalky solution of barium, but with limited accuracy.

Recently, however, technology has taken a leap forwards. In 1981, Israeli physician, Dr Gavriel Iddan, began development of a video camera that would fit inside a pill. It took 20 years for technology to catch up with him and it sounds like science fiction, but the new technique, called 'wireless capsule endoscopy', comprises a tiny, vitamin-sized capsule weighing just under 4 gm containing a colour video camera and a wireless radiofrequency transmitter, four light emitting diode (LED) lights, and enough battery power to take 50,000 colour images during an eight-hour journey through the digestive tract (Figure 1.3).

The capsule is swallowed or placed in the top of the gastrointestinal tract under anaesthetic and a belt worn on the waist captures the transmitted pictures of the entire system, top to bottom as the camera passes through it and is evacuated with a bowel movement.

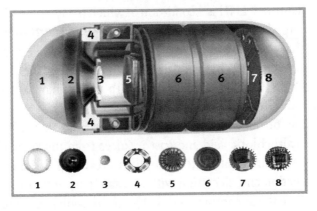

Figure 1.3 The PillCam™[1]. 1. Optical dome; 2. Lens holder; 3. Lens; 4. Illuminating light emitting diodes (LEDs); 5. Complementary metal oxide semiconductor (CMOS) image; 6. Battery; 7. Application specific integrated circuit (ASIC) transmitter; 8. Antenna. Dimensions: height 11 mm; width 26 mm; weight 3.7 gm[AQ]

This technology is proving to be very useful in identifying the source of disease in the gastrointestinal tract. For example, intestinal bleeding can cause severe anaemia and may well be

1   Pillcam™ is a registered trademark of Given Imaging Ltd.

occurring within the area of the small bowel hitherto impenetrable.

Specific gastrointestinal findings in ASD children and adults

Abnormalities have been found throughout the whole of the gastrointestinal system starting in the mouth with ulcers, then in the throat, where lymphonodular hyperplasia (LNH) has been identified. LNH is a condition in which the lymph nodes are enlarged as a normal immunological response to something that the body hasn't expected, such as food allergens, virus or bacteria. What is different with the ASD patients is that this LNH seems to be chronic, with the immune system constantly fired up.

Many of the children and adults suffer from acid reflux, when hydrochloric acid and gastric juices from the stomach flow backwards into the oesophagus causing irritation, inflammation and ulceration with resultant pain and discomfort. When this is chronic it's called gastro-oesophageal reflux disease or GERD for short. This is a symptom of the body not being able to move food properly through the digestive system and is quite a common finding.

The oesophagus is often abnormal, displaying clusters of a type of white blood cells called 'eosinophils'; when these are excessive the condition is called 'eosinophilic oesophagitis'.

If the lining of the oesophagus is exposed to the acid over years, untreated, it may develop into a condition called 'Barrett's oesophagus'. The epithelium, the mucosal cells lining the oesophagus, are replaced by columnar cells called 'Barrett's mucosa'. This is a pre-malignant state which can develop into cancer of the oesophagus. Previously unheard of in children, Barrett's oesophagus is increasingly being found in ASD children, suggesting excessive reflux or an inflammatory response or both.

In addition to the above, findings in ASD children and adults have included ulcers and inflammatory polyps in the colon, inflammation and LNH of the ileum, erosive and aphthous (small) ulcers throughout the small bowel, lymphoid hyperplasia and multiple aphthous ulcers in the duodenum, multiple duodenal peptic ulcers and stomach ulceration. Classic Crohn's disease and ulcerative colitis have also been diagnosed but these, together with coeliac disease, seem to be much rarer in the ASD population.

If a diagnosis has already been made, then there are a number of steps you can take to make everyone's life easier!

2

How You Can Help:
Five Steps to Success

1. Recognize and document the symptoms.

2. Ensure easy or frequent access to the toilet.

3. Find a way to communicate pain or need for toilet.

4. Assure dignity and eradicate bullying.

5. Effective ASD toilet training.

1. Recognize and document the symptoms

By now, you have a basic idea of the symptoms of gut disease. If you are a teacher reading this you will also have a clear picture of the children in your own class and may even be starting to think that one or two merit closer examination.

A good start is to begin looking for patterns of behaviour because you may have to interpret on behalf of the child. The more obvious physical symptoms need documenting to identify severity or regularity and so on, whilst the less obvious symptoms need identifying.

It's important for teachers and respite services to work with parents or carers to create a plan. In the best interests of the child, *everyone* has to be on the look out for patterns and potential symptoms *at all times*. Ideally, the chart you create will be with the input of the whole team both at school and at home and, as well as constantly monitoring for patterns, you should fix a date to discuss the findings as a group.

Begin by making up a simple chart of bowel movements, consistency, colour, smell, frequency, amount passed and behaviour leading up to and following the movement.

You might find the Bristol Stool Chart or Bristol Stool Scale useful. This is a medical aid designed to classify faeces into seven groups. Developed by Heaton and Lewis at the University of Bristol, it was first published in the *Scandinavian Journal of Gastroenterology* in 1997. As gastroenterologists worldwide now use this scale it will be a very useful aid when talking to the doctor. The categories are shown in Figure 2.1.

Make sure you have a column for urine as well and make sure that the chart is filled in at school, in respite and whilst the child is at home; it's *really* important to act as a team.

If the child isn't toilet-trained this will be a good starting point. It's important to consider that irrespective of any developmental reasons why an autism spectrum disorder (ASD) child is not out of pads, inflammatory bowel disease can be so devastating that there is no way a child can have any idea of when a bowel movement is about to occur. Remember, too, that this can also affect bladder control.

Neurotypical children who suffer with Crohn's disease and/or colitis cite the fact that they have to go to the toilet suddenly, often with little or no warning, as the single most difficult symptom to cope with outside the home and especially in the school setting. The lack of feeling prior to a bowel movement and/or urination is also often described. This, combined with communication deficits, makes for a very frustrating and painful situation for the ASD child with gastrointestinal problems.

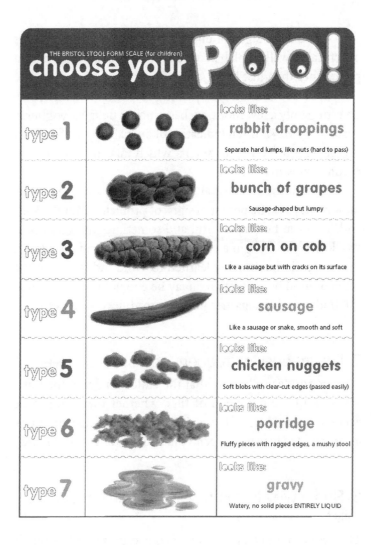

Figure 2.1 The Bristol Stool Chart. Concept by Professor DCA Candy and Emma Davey based on the Bristol Stool Form Scale produced by Dr K.W. Heaton, Reader in Medicine at the University of Bristol. Copyright © 2005 Norgine Pharmaceuticals Limited.

Look out for signs of unusual tiredness, rubbing the legs or refusal to walk, which may be indicative of associated joint pain rather than just being difficult!

Pay close attention to any eating abnormalities. Insistence on eating only a few foods, such as chicken nuggets, yoghurts, pasta or cheese, is often indicative of an inability to efficiently digest certain food components which may, in turn, lead to chronic constipation.

Not wanting to eat at all or not wanting anything in the mouth, may also be potential signs of problems. Mouth ulcers and sores can be very painful and sometimes the very act of swallowing will begin a chain of severe pain and discomfort that the child has quickly learned to avoid. Additionally, the smell of food being prepared may be enough to cause pain as the body produces gastric juices in readiness for digestion.

2. Ensure easy or frequent access to the toilet

It's a good idea to be sure that the child can get to the toilet easily, with the minimum of fuss, whether they have to be accompanied or not. Be sensitive to the fact that the more aware child may want to spend time on the toilet, 'just in case'.

3. Find a way to communicate pain or need for toilet

This works both ways and can, of course, present a huge challenge for all concerned. The fact that you are now in a position to recognize potential physical signs of underlying bowel disease in the ASD child gives you a tremendous start.

Now you are going to translate this knowledge to communicate at whatever level the child is working at. You are going to begin the process to ensure that you understand the child's needs and he or she understands that you understand!

The concept of pain is often a difficult one and there is evidence that ASD children and adults often don't experience pain in exactly the same way as other people. The key is to find a way of communicating that you understand and know that there's a problem; you may be using The Picture Exchange Communication System (PECS), the Treatment and Education of Autistic and Related Communication-handicapped CHildren (TEACCH) method or your own symbols but work on it and schedule it in very regularly. Use whatever works for each child or adult with the number one aim of empowering the individual to communicate when he or she feels some sort of urge to go to the toilet and remain sensitive to the cues. Remember that if you are using language and expecting a response then the delay in processing will mean a delayed response. Fill in the pain chart in the Resources on a regular basis to help identify the levels of pain and what may or may not be helping like a new medication or change of diet.

4. Assure dignity and eradicate bullying

It's very important for the dignity of the individual that all accidents are treated without fuss or indication of disapproval. It's also very important to think ahead to identify potentially embarrassing situations; for example on days out or school outings you should carry out a 'dignity analysis' as well as a risk analysis. Make sure that as well as wipes, gloves and so on, you always carry supplies of suitable extra clothing. How would you like it if you had to wear someone else's underpants to go home in?

The constellation of symptoms described includes a host of potential humour for other children, funny for everyone except the child who has to cringe and suffer the embarrassment of not knowing when it'll happen again. Be on the look out for other children calling names, making faces and generally bullying the child with these problems. At school, agree a protocol for handling the situation within the bullying manifesto and ensure all members of staff, including the dinner ladies and playground supervisors, are aware of how to handle the problem.

5. Effective ASD toilet training

This is a big subject, ranging from the young, non-verbal ASD child still in pads to the attention deficit hyperactivity disorder (ADHD) adolescent who has toileting accidents and all points in between. Every child is different and their ASD will manifest in differing ways too.

What you can be sure, is that it is in the interests of everyone to aim for the best possible level of toilet training for many reasons: socialization, dignity, inclusion, convenience and I'm sure you can think of many more.

Whilst best practice has to aim for reliable toilet training from the earliest possible age, the possibility that an underlying medical condition is hindering everyone's efforts must always be taken into the equation. Inevitably, some individuals will never achieve totally reliable toileting and in the case of the child with ASD, the possibility of inflammatory bowel disease (IBD) must be considered where difficulties present themselves.

It may also be that some children with ASD are hindered in their toilet training because of sensory issues, which are often a feature of the condition. Irrespective of whether or not the child suffers from IBD, sensory integration difficulties may mean that he or she cannot establish the relationship between sensation and function. The sounds and sensations of the toilet may be overwhelming and frightening to an ASD child who may 'shut down' with fear. Additionally, the sudden exposure of skin might mean that there is an unexpected response to the change in temperature.

Where a child has serious difficulty in the ability to communicate and understand language, the words *toilet, potty, pants, dry* may not be meaningful hence the absolute need to find a method of communication. A further block may be the sequencing difficulties often featured in ASD. The steps required for successful toileting and staying focused to completion are many and the challenge is enormous.

The school might not consider toilet training to be part of its remit. If this is the case it is essential that the issue be tackled at the outset and should be included in the child's individual education plan. Consider how much time a child spends at school, as opposed to how much waking time he or she spends at home and it becomes clear that a toileting programme must span both if it has any chance of succeeding.

To achieve the best possible outcome for the child, family, school and respite care must work on the project as a team.

It's always useful if the child is indicating readiness in some way. Is there any sort of indication of awareness of soiling or being wet? Is there regularity and is he or she dry for significant periods? Also, does he or she pause whilst wetting or soiling? If none of these apply then it's worth reconsidering and waiting a little while longer.

The process should be undertaken realistically and positively in the understanding that totally independent toileting may be a long way down the road. Each step in the process should be celebrated as real progress.

So you need to start by establishing a baseline, finding out when, on average, the child urinates and defecates. For three or four days take the child to the toilet every half-hour for a check to see if he or she has soiled or wet themselves.

Complete a toileting chart (see Resources) and mark down all the times, then work out the average number of times the child passes a motion or urinates during the waking day. At this stage you may begin to notice some of the symptoms of gastrointestinal disorder. If so, now is the time to bring them to the attention of the team and decide what action to take. If all's well, set up a schedule to take the child to the toilet twice as many times as the average you've worked out.

Always indicate to the child *visually* where you are going by using the sign, symbol or picture system of choice. When you get there and are installed don't stay put much beyond five minutes and, if you get a result, then provide *lots* of positive reinforcement, *lots* of praise.

One of the most successful techniques involves task analysis, in which each task is broken down by element and practised individually. So the tasks involved in going to the toilet might be:

1. Go to the toilet/bathroom.

2. Open door.

3. Undo trousers.

4. Hold trousers at waist.

5. Pull trousers down.

6. Sit down on the toilet.

7. Pass a motion.

8. Take a piece of toilet paper.

9. Wipe bottom.

10. Stand up.

11. Throw toilet paper in toilet.

12. Pull trousers up to calves.

13. Pull trousers up to thighs.

14. Pull trousers up to waist.

15. Flush the toilet.

16. Go to sink.

17. Put plug in.

18. Turn tap on.

19. Turn tap off.

20. Soap hands.

21. Wash hands.

22. Pull plug out.

23. Locate towel.

24. Dry hands.

25. Leave bathroom/toilet.

26. Close door.

For each of these tasks you will need to use a visual cue appropriate to the individual: a symbol, a photograph or even an object.

There are a number of well-documented approaches, but when there is a possibility of bowel disease be sure to bear in mind the reasons why a child may be displaying certain behaviour. For example, an aversion to entering the bathroom might be attributed to a fear of water, the noise or terror of where it goes when the toilet is flushed or perhaps the association with the severe pain it means when a bowel movement is being passed.

Before you begin, complete the basic symptoms checklist in the Resources to see if there are any areas of concern before embarking on a toilet training programme.

3

Case Histories

There follow two simplified case histories, both real case examples, demonstrating the decline of an individual and highlighting relevant symptoms on the way.

Both cases are of boys who are now grown; one is a young adolescent and the other has just left his teens. Whilst it would be impossible and unwise to try to predict the course of gastrointestinal disease in any one autism spectrum disorder (ASD)-diagnosed child it remains interesting to note the similarities in the cases and the course of the disease as it progresses.

Inflammatory bowel disease (IBD) is a relatively new phenomenon in children, which may explain why the warning signs are frequently missed by physicians. Additionally, it is also on the rise in young adults. With the added difficulties that many ASD children and adults have in interpreting and communicating their pain, parents, carers, teachers, respite workers and therapists should be on constant look out for tell-tale signs of pain and physical decline associated with IBD or any gastrointestinal complaint, from chronic constipation to retained gas.

In the UK, the government includes gastrointestinal investigations as part of the national framework for diagnosis of autism spectrum disorders, so it is hoped that more children will be spared the ongoing trauma of being left untreated for the length of time that the boys in the two case histories were.

As in non-ASD children and adults, the disease sometimes progresses to such an extent that invasive surgery is required. Ongoing research into the causes of and potential predisposition to, the condition will result in earlier diagnosis and better treatment.

Timeline Case 1

Pregnancy	Normal
0 months	Good size baby 8 lb 7oz
	Breech + normal birth
	High APGAR* score
	Easy to feed
2 weeks	Thrush in groin
6 weeks	Stopped breast-feeding
6 months	Sat up
	Weaned to homemade food
	Good appetite/diet
8½ months	Influenza
9 months	Temporary loose bowel movements
10 months	Ear infection – right ear bled
	Crawled

Thriving baby
Growth normal
All milestones met

* Appearance, Pulse, Grimace, Activity and Respiration (APGAR)

12 months	Walked
13 months	No babbling yet
3 years	Potty trained
3½ years	Dry day and night
4 years	Autism diagnosed
4½ years	Red lips
	Patting mouth
	Faeces seeping out of bottom
	Soft clay-like red brown stools
	Chemical ammonia-like smell
	Lost bladder control
	Glazed eyes
	Terrible thirst
5 years	Started refusing foods
	Rejected foods previously enjoyed
8 years	Started to lose weight
	Behaviour deteriorated
	Began dietary intervention
	Outcome:
8 years	• behaviour much improved • good natured/no aggression • bowels better • gas much reduced
10 years	2 St 8 lb
	Self-limiting food

Stopped drinking

Dietary intervention revoked

Outcome
- major aggressive outbursts

10½ years   Thrush

Balanitis

Developed terror of eating

Severe fissures in mouth

Tongue white with thrush

Haemorrhaged from rectum twice

13 years   Investigated by gastroenterologist

Upper endoscopy

PillCam™

'Carpet' of small ulcers in small bowel

Colitis of large bowel + severe reflux

Immediate treatment:
- steroids
- mesalazine
- Zantac®

Outcome:
- growth
- muscle replacement
- shoe size + 2 sizes in 3 months
- hair glossy
- happy child
- Accessing activities,
  e.g. pony riding, swimming,
  hiking, basketball, dog walking

Case 1 discussion

This timeline is of a young man whose life began very normally. Following an easy, trouble-free pregnancy, his birth, despite being breech, was uneventful and his APGAR score high. He experienced common ailments of thrush in his groin, together with an ear infection and despite a bout of influenza was a happy, bouncing baby.

He thrived until 13 months old when concern was raised that he was not babbling, although his other common milestones of walking, crawling and potty training were adequately met.

At four and a half years of age his physical health deteriorated rapidly and his bladder control was lost. A number of physical symptoms were immediately suggestive of an inflammatory bowel condition but were not recognized as such by local doctors and his behaviour became unmanageable.

Dietary intervention at eight years of age helped a great deal with the behaviour issues and marginally with the bowel symptoms but, by age ten, despite repeated efforts by the parents to make local medics understand the severity of his physical condition his weight had plummeted to 2st 8lb and he had begun to refuse both food and drink. The appearance of severe oral fissures together with two episodes of rectal haemorrhaging led eventually to appropriate investigation by a fully qualified gastroenterologist.

The results showed ulceration throughout the small bowel and colitis of the large bowel. Whilst the gastric area was clear, the severe reflux continued to cause extreme pain and discomfort.

Following immediate treatment with antacids, steroids and anti-inflammatory agents this young man's health improved rapidly. His shoe size increased by two sizes in three months and he began to replace lost muscle. His hair became glossy and he is able to access all manner of outdoor activities, which he enjoys greatly. His family reports that his quality of life is improved beyond measure. He remains on appropriate medication for his bowel disease whilst the residual complaint is of continued dry, cracked lips.

Timeline Case 2

Pregnancy	Normal
0 months	Good size baby 8 lb 10 oz
	Normal birth
	Very high APGAR score
	Easy to feed
6 months	Sat up
	Mix baby food/breast
	Good appetite/diet
10 months	Crawled
12 months	Walked
16 months	Upper respiratory tract infection
	Diarrhoea and vomiting x 7 days
20 months	Stopped breast-feeding
	Recurrent rashes on bottom
	Septic spots on legs
	Respiratory tract infections
20 months	
26 months	Losing speech
28 months	Night waking

Thriving baby
Growth normal
All milestones met

	Screaming and head-banging
30 months	Temper tantrums began
	Terrible thirst
32 months	Lost all interest in toys
	Loss of all understanding of speech
	Physical deterioration
	Constant diarrhoea
	Recurring ear infections
34 months	Dietary intervention
	Outcomes:
	• hyperactivity reduced
	• concentration better
	• behaviour more manageable
	• sociability improved
	• verbal development
	Not toilet trained
36 months	Hayfever developed
	Weight loss observed
3½ years	High pollen count affects gut function
	Ongoing diarrhoea
4½ years	More weight loss
	Serious loss of awareness
	Major loss of function
5 years	Deficiencies in:
	• zinc, magnesium, manganese
	• B12, iron
	Supplements and B12 injections

	Improvements
6 years	Ongoing infections of upper respiratory tract/ears
	Diarrhoea
	Autism suggested
	Gut bacteria introduced
7 years	Gastrointestinal investigations

Findings:

- lymphonodular hyperplasia (LNH)
- apthoid ulcers
- low-grade IBD
- abnormalities in terminal ileum

Treatment:

- non-steroidal anti-inflammatory agents
- specialized IBD feed

Outcome:
- behaviour much improved
- limited understanding/ language
- bowels better
- became 95 per cent toilet trained
- still highly sensitive to many foods
- able to enjoy life/education
- no aggression
- residual motility impairment

Treatment:
- ongoing medication

Case 2 discussion

This timeline is also of a young man whose life began normally. Following an easy, trouble-free pregnancy, his birth, on the due date, was uneventful and his APGAR score exceptionally high.

At 16 months old he suffered from a bout of diarrhoea and vomiting, which lasted for seven days and at 20 months he stopped breast-feeding, following which he began to suffer from many infections.

His milestones until 20 months of age were met and whilst he had begun to suffer from physical ailments, his cognitive development was not in question until the end of his second year when concern was raised that he was losing speech.

By 28 months, his behaviour was beginning to become difficult and his sleep pattern was disrupted with a great deal of night waking and head-banging. His physical health deteriorated consistently over the following months, as did his understanding.

Local doctors did not recognize the signs of IBD and by five years of age, despite a good dietary intake, he was showing serious deficits in vitamins and minerals essential for brain development.

As in Case 1, dietary intervention helped a great deal with the behavioural issues but only marginally with the bowel symptoms which were not resolved until the age of eight.

The results of the gastrointestinal investigations showed widespread lymphonodular hyperplasia (LNH) with patchy ulceration in the small bowel.

Following treatment with anti-inflammatory agents and specialized formula for IBD providing easily digestible minerals and vitamins, this young man's health gradually returned. He no longer suffers from the upper respiratory tract infections which had plagued him and is far more tolerant of pollen.

He remains highly sensitive to many foods which can cause diarrhoea and behavioural problems if ingested and suffers residual motility problems which require constant medication to avoid constipation. He has developed seizures which are made worse by constipation.

Overall, the treatment he received has ensured that he remains comfortable and pain-free whilst permitting him to take part in activities normal for his age despite his severe autism.

4

Treatment of Gastrointestinal Complaints

If gastrointestinal investigations have identified bowel disease, the treatment goal is to reduce and banish the inflammation, and kill any unwanted germs and parasites that may be in the intestines. Replace the bad bacteria with good ones and control the disease in order to prevent flare-ups as much as possible.

Diarrhoea and constipation have to be kept in check as well.

The gastroenterologist will prescribe different treatment according to the severity of the findings. Non-steroidal anti-inflammatory agents, steroids and immunosuppressive drugs may all be used to reduce the inflammation, whilst antibiotics may be prescribed to kill off specific germs.

Many, but not all, autism spectrum disorder (ASD) children and adults react adversely to some foodstuffs and dietary intervention, if not already part of the patient's treatment regimen, may well be advised.

An elemental diet may be prescribed: this is a formula which provides all the essential nutrients for brain and body function, broken down into a form that can be easily assimilated and absorbed through the damaged gut.

Impacted faeces not only need to be cleared out prior to investigation but also have to be kept at bay by use of a drug to assist gut motility and prevent recurrent build-up.

The impactions are frequently hard and a softening agent may be required before they can be completely cleared out of the system. Sometimes this type of medication is all that is needed to maintain an even flow through the system whilst others require an ongoing laxative preparation or even a combination of both.

It is essential to ensure that whatever drug is used is free from artificial sweeteners, flavours and colourings as these can exacerbate the condition in the sensitive ASD child or adult. Discuss these issues with the doctor, who will indicate the sensitivities on the prescription. The pharmacist may then source suitable preparations.

It is useful to ensure that all the doctors involved in the care of the child or adult are working together to understand the total picture. For example, the allergy specialist may not realize that a high pollen count can exacerbate the gut problems or the general practitioner may not make a connection between potential signs of arthritis and inflammatory bowel disease.

It's always a good idea to take a complete list of the names and addresses of all the different doctors and therapists involved in your charge's care. When you have a medical appointment take a copy of the list for the doctor and ask that any correspondence be copied to you and all of them as well.

5

Resources

The following three charts and a checklist are included to assist in behaviour and pain analysis.

Toileting and behaviour chart

As an assessment tool, the toileting and behaviour chart should be filled in daily. This will provide a visual way of identifying any connection between behaviours, bowel and bladder movements and eating and drinking. The header row shows a list of activities and reactions whilst the side bar indicates the time of day in hours.

For each hour of the day, simply tick any relevant box. In order to establish whether or not any pattern exists, it is advisable to complete this chart over a minimum four-week period.

Pain chart

The pain chart on page 56 lists the most commonly observed behaviours and symptoms which have been associated with bowel disorders and bowel disease. This should be completed in tandem with the toileting and behaviour chart to provide a more quantitative assessment.

Each observation is scored according to whether it seemed to have happened a great deal, quite a lot, a little, or not at all. Circle the appropriate number in each row or put a tick in the 'Can't tell' box then add up the score at the bottom.

Comparing both charts over a period of time presents an extremely useful picture. As the days go by it becomes possible to spot patterns. For example, a child might be passing a motion every three days and the score on the pain chart might rise until the bowels have been evacuated.

Toilet training chart

The toilet training chart on page 57 provides a visual of how frequently the bowels and bladder are being opened, establishing whether or not there is a pattern and whether the toilet has been used or not.

For every day of the week whenever the bowels or bladder are opened, fill in the appropriate box, either *toilet* or *underpants* (read 'pad' here if appropriate), with a B for a bowel movement or a U for urination.

TOILETING AND BEHAVIOUR CHART

Name:

Day:

Date:

Time	Bowels opened	Urinated	Aggression	Hyperactivity	Screaming	Giggling	Obvious pain	Absences	Responsiveness	Food	Drink
7.00											
8.00											
9.00											
10.00											
11.00											
12.00											
1.00											
2.00											
3.00											
4.00											
5.00											
6.00											
7.00											
8.00											
9.00											
10.00											
11.00											
12.00											

PAIN CHART

Name:

Day:

Date:

OBSERVATIONS	Not at All	A Little	Quite a Lot	A Great Deal	Can't Tell	Score
Adopted Strange Postures	0	1	2	3		
Aggressive	0	1	2	3		
Self-Harmed	0	1	2	3		
Reluctant to eat	0	1	2	3		
Frowned/furrowed brow	0	1	2	3		
Looked frightened	0	1	2	3		
Agitated/restless	0	1	2	3		
Touching or rubbing parts of body	0	1	2	3		
Grinding teeth	0	1	2	3		
Disturbed sleep	0	1	2	3		
Pulled away/flinched on being touched	0	1	2	3		
Appeared withdrawn or depressed	0	1	2	3		
Stereotypical movements	0	1	2	3		
Hyperactive	0	1	2	3		
Grimaced/screwed up eyes or face	0	1	2	3		
Had seizures	0	1	2	3		
Cried/moaned/whimpered	0	1	2	3		
						TOTAL

TOILET TRAINING CHART

Name:

Start Day:

Start Date:

TIME	DAY 1		DAY 2		DAY 3		DAY 4		DAY 5		DAY 6		DAY 7	
	Underpants	Toilet	Underpants	Toilet	Underpants	Toilet	Underpants	Toilet	Underpants	Toilet	Underpants	Toilet	Underpants	Toilet
7.00														
8.00														
9.00														
10.00														
11.00														
12.00														
1.00														
2.00														
3.00														
4.00														
5.00														
6.00														
7.00														
8.00														
9.00														

Enter U for urine and B for bowel movement

Basic symptoms checklist

Review this list and tick any relevant boxes. Once done this will provide a helpful starting point to begin discussions with the doctor responsible for treatment. Copies of all the completed charts will also provide useful information to begin a dialogue with the whole medical, educational and therapeutic team.

The following symptoms, which doctors would call 'clinical manifestations', may indicate that a child or adult with autism spectrum disorder (ASD) may be suffering from an underlying gastrointestinal problem. These symptoms should be taken seriously and should be investigated by a gastroenterologist.

- Diarrhoea
- Constipation
- Alternating diarrhoea/constipation
- Flatulence
- Malodorous stools
- Undigested food in stools
- Grainy stools
- Adopting strange positions when on the toilet
- Adopting strange positions during the day
- Constant screaming
- Hands down trousers
- Clutching the stomach
- Urinary incontinence
- Frequent bowel accidents
- Abdominal distension

- Unusually small for age
- Unusually skinny for age
- Behaviour better after passing motion
- Mucous in stools/pants
- Blood in stools/pants
- Infrequent stools
- Blocked toilet bowls
- Stools like rabbit droppings
- Long stringy stools
- Unformed stools
- Behaviour aggressive before passing a motion
- Behaviour noticeably better after passing a motion

Glossary

This is a basic list of definitions of medical terms you may come across in the medical care of autism spectrum disorder (ASD) children and adults who experience gastro-enterological complaints.

5-ASA 5-aminosalicylic acid or mesalazine; 5-ASA is delivered to the small and large intestine where it is active against the inflammation seen in inflammatory bowel disease.

Abscess A localized collection of pus in a cavity formed by the decay of diseased tissues.

Acute Sudden onset of symptoms (as in an inflammatory bowel disease (IBD) relapse).

Aetiology Cause.

Anaemia A reduction in the number of red blood cells in the body, which results in insufficient oxygen being carried by the blood to the organs of the body.

Anastomosis The joining together of two ends of healthy bowel after diseased bowel has been cut out (resected) by the surgeon.

Ankylosing spondylitis Chronic inflammatory disease of the spine and nearby joints which can cause pain and stiffness in the spine, neck, hips, jaw and rib cage.

Anus The opening to the back passage.

Arthralgia Pains in the joints.

Arthritis Inflammation of a joint(s) causing pain, swelling and stiffness.

Ascending colon The portion of bowel extending from the caecum to the hepatic flexure.

Autistic enterocolitis New variant of inflammatory bowel disease found in children on the autistic spectrum and other developmental disorders.

Balloon catheter An inflatable plastic cylinder mounted on a thin tube and used for dilating narrowed areas of the intestine.

Biopsy Removal of small pieces of tissue from parts of the body (e.g. colon – colonic biopsy) for examination under the microscope to diagnose disease or determine disease progression.

Bulk laxative see laxative.

Caecum The first part of the large intestine. It is a blind-ending pouch at the junction between the small and large intestines.

Chronic Symptoms occurring over a long period of time.

Cobblestoning Characteristic appearance of the intestinal lining in Crohn's disease. The 'cobblestone' effect is the result of deep ulceration and swelling of the surrounding tissue.

Coeliac disease Inflammation of the intestinal tract caused by an autoimmune response to gluten.

Colitis Inflammation of the colon.

Colon The large intestine. It extends from the caecum to the rectum and has ascending, transverse and descending portions.

Colonoscopy Inspection of the colon by an illuminated flexible tube called a 'colonoscope'.

Colostomy Surgical creation of an opening between the colon and the surface of the body. Part of the colon is brought out on to the abdomen to create a stoma. A bag is placed over this to collect waste material.

Constipation Infrequency or difficulty in the passage of bowel motions.

Corticosteroids Natural substances produced by the body that act against the inflammation seen in inflammatory bowel disease.

Crohn's disease activity index (CDAI) Measurement of the severity of active disease using symptom scores that are monitored over one week.

CT scan Computerized tomography scan. A specialized form of X-ray examination that produces cross-sectional images of the body.

Defaecation The act of passing faeces.

Descending colon The portion of bowel between the splenic flexure and the sigmoid colon.

Diarrhoea An increase in frequency, liquidity and weight of bowel motions (normal production <200 g in 24 hours).

Distal Further down the bowel towards the anus.

Diverticulum (plural diverticula) Small pouch-like projection(s) in the wall of the intestine; may become infected, causing diverticulitis.

Dysplasia Alteration in size, shape and organization of mature cells, possible development of cancer.

Dysuria Pain on urination.

Electrolytes Salts in the blood, e.g. sodium, potassium, calcium.

Endoscopy A collective name for all visual inspections of body cavities with an illuminated flexible tube. Examples are colonoscopy and sigmoidoscopy.

Enema A liquid (e.g. barium) introduced into the rectum for treatment, diagnostic purposes or to stimulate the production of a bowel motion.

Erythema nodosum Red, tender swellings occasionally seen on the shins and lower legs during a flare-up of inflammatory bowel disease. They usually subside when the disease is in remission.

Erythrocytes Red cells in the blood that carry oxygen.

Exacerbation An aggravation of symptoms.

Faeces The waste matter eliminated from the body through the anus (other names are 'stools' and 'motions').

Fibre optic Flexible fibres that carry light, e.g. in a colonoscope.

Fissure A cleft or groove (crack) in the surface of the skin.

Fistula An abnormal connection, usually between two organs or leading from an internal organ to the surface of the body.

Flatus Gas from the rectum.

Fulminant colitis Colitis occurring suddenly with great intensity and severity.

Gastroenteritis Inflammation of the stomach and intestine.

Granulomas Nodules of cells, surrounded by lymphocytes, which can be found in all layers of the bowel. If present, they strongly suggest Crohn's disease.

Haematochezia The passage of bloody stools.

Haemorrhoids Swollen veins in the area of the anus. They bleed easily and are often painful.

Harvey and Bradshaw Index Simple measurement of disease activity in Crohn's disease measured over a 24-hour period.

Hepatic flexure Part of the colon where the ascending and transverse portions meet, below the liver.

Heredity The transmission of characteristics from parent to child.

Histology The examination of tissues under the microscope to assist diagnosis.

Hypoalbuminaemia Decreased levels of albumin (protein) in the blood.

Hypokalaemia Decreased levels of potassium in the blood.

Ileal/ileo Of the ileum (as in ileocolitis).

Ileo–anal anastomosis The surgical joining of the end of the ileum to the anus to bypass the colon.

Ileostomy This is when the open end of the healthy ileum is diverted to the surface of the abdomen and secured there to form a new exit for waste matter.

Ileum The lowest part of the small intestine.

Immune response The body's reaction to invasion by foreign substances; it involves inflammation of the affected part of the body.

Immunosuppressed A person's immune response is not activated by a foreign substance.

Inflammation The body's natural defence mechanism in which blood rushes to any site of damage or infection causing reddening, swelling and pain. The area is usually hot to touch.

Iritis Painful inflammation of the iris in the eyes.

Laxative An agent that acts to cause emptying of the bowel. This may be by purging (irritating the lining) or increasing the volume of stool (bulking).

Lesion A term used to describe any structural abnormality in the body.

Leucocytes White cells in the blood that help fight infection.

Leucocytosis An increase in the number of circulating white cells in the blood.

Leucopenia A decrease in the number of circulating white cells in the blood.

Lymphocytes A particular kind of leucocyte.

Lymphonodular hyperplasia (LNH) Enlarged and inflamed lymphoid nodules.

MRI scan Magnetic resonance imaging scan. A diagnostic technique that uses high-frequency radio waves and a computer to visualize the organs of the body. It does not use potentially harmful X-rays.

Mucous A white, slimy lubricant produced by the intestines. It is found in excess in the stools of patients with colitis.

Nausea Feeling sick.

Oedema Accumulation (build-up) of excessive amounts of fluid in the tissues resulting in swelling.

Osteoporosis Weakening of the bones due to calcium loss. May be caused by long-term use of steroids or low levels of the hormones oestrogen or testosterone.

Pathogen Harmful organism causing disease.

Pathology The study of the cause and progress of disease.

Perforation An abnormal opening (hole) in the wall of the bowel that causes the contents of the bowel to spill into the abdominal cavity.

Peri-anal Around the anus.

Peritoneum The membrane lining the abdominal cavity.

Peritonitis Inflammation of the peritoneum, often caused by a perforation.

Polyp A protruding growth from the lining of the intestine (e.g. colonic polyp – a polyp in the colon).

Pouch A surgical enlargement of an ileo–anal anastomosis to form the equivalent of a rectum.

Pouchitis Inflammation of a pouch.

Proctitis Inflammation of the rectum.

Prophylaxis Treatment to prevent a disease occurring before it has started.

Proximal Further up the bowel towards the mouth.

Pyoderma gangrenosum A type of chronic skin ulceration that sometimes occurs on the limbs of people with inflammatory bowel disease.

Radiologist A specialist who interprets X-ray pictures to make a diagnosis.

Rectosigmoid area The junction between the sigmoid colon and the rectum.

Rectum The lowest 20 cm of the large intestine, just above the anus.

Relapse Return of disease activity.

Remission Absence of symptoms of the disease and return to good health.

Sacroileitis Inflammation of the joint between the backbone and the pelvic bone.

Sigmoid colon The portion of the colon shaped like the letters 'S' or 'C', extending from the descending colon to the rectum.

Sigmoidoscopy Inspection of the sigmoid colon with an illuminated tube called a sigmoidoscope.

Skip lesions Areas of inflammation with areas of normal intestinal lining in between (seen in Crohn's disease).

Splenic flexure That portion of the colon where the transverse and the descending colon meet, below the spleen.

Steatorrhoea Presence of excess fat in the faeces.

Stoma Artificial opening of the intestine through the abdominal surface. Created by surgery.

Stricture The narrowing of a portion of the bowel.

Suppository A smooth-shaped solid medication inserted into the rectum.

Tenesmus Persistent urge to empty the bowel, caused by an inflamed rectum.

Terminal ileum The last part of the ileum, where the small intestine joins the large intestine.

Total parental nutrition (TPN) When the whole diet (i.e. all necessary nutrients) is delivered by injection into a vein.

Toxic megacolon A dilatation (swelling) of the colon that may lead to perforation, usually resulting in a very severe attack of ulcerative colitis or Crohn's disease. Urgent surgery is almost always needed.

Transverse colon The portion of bowel between the hepatic and splenic flexures.

Tumour An abnormal growth that may be benign (non-cancerous) or malignant (cancerous).

Ultrasound Use of high-pitched sound waves to produce pictures of internal organs on a screen for diagnostic purposes.

Uveitis Inflammation of that part of the eye that regulates the amount of light entering the eye.

Bibliography

Afazal, N., Murch, S., Thirrupathy, K., Berger, L., Fagbemi, A. and Heuschkel, R. (2003) 'Constipation with acquired magarectum in children with autism.' *Pediatrics 112*, 939–942.

Ashwood, P., Anthony, A., Pellicer, A.A., Torrente, F., Walker-Smith, J.A. and Wakefield, A.J. (2003) 'Intestinal lymphocyte populations in children with regressive autism: evidence for extensive mucosal immunopathology.' *Journal of Clinical Immunology 23*, 504–517.

Atkinson, W., Sheldon, T.A., Shaath, N. and Whorwell, P.J. (2004) 'Food elimination based on IgG antibodies in irritable bowel syndrome: a randomised controlled trial.' *Gut 53*, 1459–1464.

Balzola, F., Barbon, V., Repici, A., Rizzetto, M. *et al.* (2005) 'Panenteric IBD-like disease in a patient with regressive autism shown for the first time by the wireless capsule enteroscopy: another piece on the jigsaw of this gut-brain syndrome?' *American Journal of Gastroenterology 100*, 979–981.

Buie, T. (1997) 'Gastrointentinal Issues Encountered in Autism.' In: M.L. Bauman and T.L. Kemper (eds) *The Neurobiology of Autism.* New York, NY: Plenum Press.

D'Eufemia, P., Celli, M., Finocchiaro, R., Pacifico. L. *et al.* (1996) 'Abnormal intestinal permeability in children with autism.' *Acta Paediatrica 85*, 1076–1079.

Finegold, S.M., Molitoris, D., Song, Y., Liu, C. *et al.* (2002) 'Gastrointestinal microflora studies in late-onset autism.' *Clinical Infectious Diseases 35(Suppl.1)*, S6–S16.

Furlano, R.I., Anthony, A., Day, R., Brown, A. *et al.* (2001) 'Colonic CD8 and gamma delta T-cell infiltration with epithelial damage in children with autism.' *Journal of Pediatrics 138*, 366–372.

Horvath, K., Papadimitriou, J.C., Rabsztyn, A., Drachenberg, C. and Tildon, J.T. (1999) 'Gastrointestinal abnormalities in children with autistic disorder.' *Journal of Pediatrics 135*, 559–563.

Jyonouchi, H., Geng, L., Ruby, A. and Zimmerman-Bier, B. (2005) 'Dysregulated innate immune responses in young children with autism spectrum disorders: their relationship to gastrointestinal symptoms and dietary intervention.' *Neuropsychobiology 51*, 77–85.

Jyonouchi, H., Geng, L., Ruby, A. and Zimmerman-Bier, B. (2005) 'Evaluation of an association between gastrointestinal symptoms and cytokine production against common dietary proteins in children with autism spectrum disorders.' *Journal of Pediatrics 146*, 605–610.

Kokkonen, J., Haapalahti, M., Tikkanen, S., Karttunen, R. and Savilahti, E. (2004) 'Gastrointestinal complaints and diagnosis in children: a population-based study.' *Acta Paediatrica 93*, 880–886.

Latchman, F., Merino, F., Lang, A., Garvey, J. *et al.* (2003) 'A consistent pattern of minor immunodeficiency and subtle enteropathy in children with multiple food allergy.' *Journal of Pediatrics 143*, 39–47.

Molloy, C.A. and Manning-Courtney, P. (2003) 'Prevalance of chronic gastrointestinal symptoms in children with autism and autistic spectrum disorders.' *Autism 7*, 165–171.

Sandler, R.H., Finegold, S.M., Bolte, E.R., Buchanan, C.P. *et al.* (2000) 'Short-term benefit from oral vancomycin treatment of regressive-onset autism.' *Journal of Child Neurology 15*, 429–435.

Torrente, F., Ashwood, P., Day, R., Machado, N. *et al.* (2002) 'Small intestinal enteropathy with epithelial IgG and complement deposition in children with regressive autism.' *Molecular Psychiatry 7*, 375–382, 334.

Torrente, F., Anthony, A., Heuschkel, R.B., Thomson, M.A., Ashwood, P. and Murch, S.H. (2004) 'Focal-enhanced gastritis in regressive autism with features distinct from Crohn's and *Helicobacter pylori* gastritis.' *American Journal of Gastroenterology 99*, 598–605.

Uhlmann, V., Martin, C.M., Sheils, O., Pilkington, L. *et al.* (2002) 'Potential viral pathogenic mechanism for new variant inflammatory bowel disease.' *Molecular Pathology 55*, 84–90.

Van Heest, R., Jones, S. and Giacomantonio, M. (2004) 'Rectal prolapse in autistic children.' *Journal of Pediatric Surgery 39*, 643–644.

Wakefield, A.J., Anthony, A., Murch, S.H., Thomson, M. *et al.* (2000) 'Enterocolitis in children with developmental disorders.' *American Journal of Gastroenterology 95*, 2285–2295.

Wakefield, A.J., Murch, S.H., Anthony, A., Linnell, J. *et al.* (1998) 'Ileal-lymphoid-nodular hyperplasia, non-specific colitis and pervasive developmental disorder in children.' *Lancet 351*, 637–641.

Wakefield, A.J., Puleston, J.M., Montgomery, S.M., Anthony, A., O'Leary, J.J. and Murch, S.H. (2002) 'Review article: the concept of entero-colonic encephalopathy, autism and opioid receptor ligands.' *Alimentary Pharmacology and Therapeutics 16*, 663–674.

Welch, M.G., Keune, J.D., Welch-Horan, T.B., Anwar, N., Anwar, M. and Ruggiero, D.A. (2003) 'Secretine activates visceral brain regions in the rat including areas abnormal in autism.' *Cellular and Molecular Neurobiology 23*, 817–837.

White, J.F. (2003) 'Intestinal pathophysiology in autism.' *Experimental Biology and Medicine 228*, 639–649.

Index